ALIEN MESSIAHS

Alien Messiahs

DANIELLE ISABELLA

Contents

Chapter 1

Introduction to UFO Beliefs and Cult Phenomena

HISTORICAL CONTEXT OF UFO BELIEFS

The historical context of UFO beliefs is deeply intertwined with societal changes, technological advancements, and cultural shifts throughout the 20th and 21st centuries. The modern UFO phenomenon began to gain traction in the post-World War II era, catalyzed by a surge in interest in aviation technology and the onset of the Cold War. This period saw the emergence of numerous sightings and reports, often fueled by the public's fascination with space exploration and the possibilities. of extraterrestrial life. Such events coincided with a growing skepticism towards traditional institutions, including government and organized religion, leading many individuals to seek alternative explanations for the unknown.

In the 1960s and 1970s, the cultural landscape underwent significant transformation, marked by countercultural movements that questioned established norms. This era saw the rise of new religious movements, many of which incorporated UFO beliefs into their teachings. Groups such as the Unarius Academy of Science and Heaven's Gate presented elaborate cosmologies that framed alien encounters as pivotal moments in human evolution and spiritual awakening. These cults often provided a sense of community and belonging for individuals disillusioned by conventional religious doctrines, tapping into the zeitgeist of the age that embraced both spiritual exploration and the quest for knowledge beyond Earth.

The influence of UFO sightings on the formation of these new religious movements cannot be overstated. Sightings often acted as catalysts for collective experiences that bonded individuals to a shared belief system. Personal testimonies of encounters with alien beings not only legitimized these experiences within the cult framework but also served as the foundation for charismatic leadership. Leaders of these movements frequently presented themselves as intermediaries between humanity and extraterrestrial civilizations, claiming special knowledge or messages from the cosmos. This dynamic often created a unique psychological profile of cult leaders who capitalized on the hopes and fears of their followers, positioning themselves as guides in a complex and uncertain world.

As the digital age emerged, the role of social media in promoting UFO-related religious groups became increasingly prominent and multifaceted. Online platforms not only facilitated the rapid dissemination of information and personal experiences but also allowed for the formation of vibrant virtual communities centered around UFO beliefs and experiences. This significant shift not only expanded the reach of existing cults but also gave rise to entirely new movements that effectively leveraged the power of online engagement and connectivity. The interconnectedness offered by social media enabled individuals from diverse backgrounds and regions to come together, often leading to an amplification and intensification of beliefs and practices that previously might have remained confined to localized areas. As a result, the landscape of UFO cults evolved dramatically, reflecting the ongoing and dynamic interplay between advancing technology and deeply held belief systems. The historical analysis of UFO cults reveals a complex and intricate interplay between societal anxieties, spiritual quests, and the ongoing search for meaning in an increasingly perplexing and chaotic world. With the advent of government disclosure initiatives regarding UFOs and unidentified aerial phenomena, the dynamics surrounding these beliefs continue to evolve and shift. The impact of such disclosures on cult membership trends raises critical and thought-provoking questions about the future of UFO-related religions and their place within the broader, multifaceted context of human spirituality. Understanding the historical context of these beliefs is essential for both researchers and enthusiasts alike, as it sheds light on the underlying psychological, sociocultural, and emotional factors that drive individuals toward extraterrestrial narratives and the communities that form around them, ultimately contributing to a richer understanding of this phenomenon.

DEFINITION AND CHARACTERISTICS OF CULTS

Cults, often defined as religious or social groups with beliefs and practices that deviate from mainstream society, exhibit distinctive characteristics that set them apart from traditional religious organizations. In the context of UFO beliefs, cults frequently emerge in response to societal anxieties and the search for meaning in an increasingly complex world. These groups typically revolve around charismatic leaders who claim to possess exclusive knowledge or insights about extraterrestrial life, often presenting themselves as intermediaries between humanity and higher, often alien, powers. This dynamic fosters a unique environment where members are encouraged to adopt new worldviews that challenge conventional thinking.

One defining characteristic of cults is their authoritarian structure, where a central figure or leadership group exerts significant control over members' beliefs and behaviors. In UFO-based cults, leaders often leverage claims of direct communication with extraterrestrial beings or advanced spiritual teachings, reinforcing their authority and fostering dependency among followers. This hierarchical dynamic can create an insular community that prioritizes loyalty to the leader and the group over critical thinking or external relationships. As members become increasingly isolated from outside influences, the potential for manipulation and psychological control intensifies.

Cults also tend to employ specific rituals and practices that reinforce their beliefs and foster a sense of belonging among members. In the realm of UFO religions, these rituals may include communal gatherings centered around shared experiences, such as UFO sightings or meditation sessions aimed at connecting with extraterrestrial entities. The symbolism associated with these practices often draws from popular culture, science fiction, and new-age spirituality, creating an amalgamation of beliefs that resonate with the participants' desire for transcendence and understanding of the unknown. These rituals serve not only as a means of reaffirming group identity but also as a method of instilling loyalty and commitment to the cult's ideologies.

The role of social media in the proliferation of UFO-related cults cannot be understated. Platforms such as Facebook, Instagram, and YouTube have become pivotal in disseminating beliefs, fostering community, and recruiting new members. The immediacy and accessibility of these platforms allow cult leaders to reach a broader audience, often employing persuasive narratives and emotional appeals that resonate with individuals seeking connection and purpose in a tumultuous world. This digital landscape has enabled the rapid spread of UFO beliefs, making it easier for like-minded individuals to find each other and form communities grounded in shared experiences and ideologies, often bypassing traditional avenues of religious or spiritual exploration.

Finally, the intersection of psychological factors and societal trends plays a crucial role in the understanding of cult dynamics within the context of UFO beliefs. Individuals drawn to these groups may be motivated by a variety of psychological needs, including a desire for belonging, a search for meaning, or an escape from societal pressures. As government disclosure regarding UFO phenomena continues to evolve, the potential impact on cult membership trends warrants careful examination. The interplay between personal testimonies, societal anxieties, and the promise of enlightenment through alien encounters creates a complex web that cultivates the formation and persistence of UFO cults in contemporary society. Understanding these dynamics offers critical insights into the psychological profiles of cult leaders and the vulnerable populations they attract.

THE INTERSECTION OF UFOS AND RELIGION

The intersection of UFOs and religion presents a unique landscape that reflects humanity's quest for meaning in an increasingly complex world. As sightings and encounters with unidentified flying objects have proliferated, they have not only sparked scientific inquiry but have also ignited spiritual movements that often draw parallels with traditional religious themes. This phenomenon is particularly pronounced in new religious movements, where the presence of extraterrestrial beings is reinterpreted through a spiritual lens, suggesting a divine purpose or intervention. Such reinterpretations challenge established religious narratives and offer adherents a sense of belonging and purpose.

The influence of UFO sightings on the emergence of new religious movements illustrates a psychological need for understanding and belonging. Cult leaders often position themselves as intermediaries between the celestial and terrestrial realms, providing followers with a framework to comprehend their experiences and the universe. This phenomenon aligns with historical patterns where charismatic leaders have emerged during times of societal upheaval. The allure of UFOs and the promise of contact with extraterrestrial intelligences can be particularly compelling in modern contexts marked by existential uncertainty, thereby facilitating the rapid growth of these groups.

Examining the psychological profiles of cult leaders within the context of UFO beliefs reveals a pattern of traits that resonate with notions of authority and messianic leadership. Many leaders exhibit exceptional charisma, coupled with a deep-seated belief in their unique insights into the extraterrestrial realm. This belief often manifests in a narrative that frames them as chosen figures destined to guide humanity towards enlightenment and salvation. Such narratives not only enhance their appeal but also serve to solidify their control over followers, who may be seeking validation of their own experiences with the unknown.

The historical analysis of cults formed around alien encounters further underscores the complex relationship between UFO sightings and religious fervor. From the early 20th century to contemporary movements, instances of mass sightings have often coincided with the rise of cults that interpret these phenomena as signs of divine presence. This historical trajectory reveals a cyclical pattern in which societal fears and hopes are projected onto the unknown, creating fertile ground for the emergence of new belief systems that offer alternative explanations for the mysteries of existence.

In the digital age, the role of social media has become pivotal in promoting UFO-related religious groups. Platforms designed for instant communication and information sharing provide a space for like-minded individuals to connect, share experiences, and propagate beliefs about extraterrestrial encounters as spiritual phenomena. This technological evolution has transformed the landscape of religious expression, allowing for rapid dissemination of ideas and practices that may not conform to traditional religious frameworks. As individuals navigate this intersection of belief and experience, the ethical implications of UFO cults in contemporary society warrant careful examination, particularly concerning the well-being of followers and the potential for exploitation by those in positions of authority.

Chapter 2

The Rise of Cults in the Era of UFO Disclosure

HISTORICAL OVERVIEW OF UFO DISCLOSURE EVENTS

The historical overview of UFO disclosure events reveals a complex interplay between government transparency, public fascination, and the emergence of new belief systems. The narrative of UFOs in the modern context began in the mid-20th century, particularly post-World War II, when a series of reported sightings and alleged encounters prompted both governmental and civilian investigations. The infamous Roswell incident in 1947 marked a pivotal moment, sparking widespread speculation about extraterrestrial life and government cover-ups. This event laid the groundwork for a burgeoning interest in UFO phenomena, leading to a series of disclosures from military personnel and civilian witnesses that would shape public perception and foster a culture of inquiry.

In the 1970s, following the establishment of organizations such as MUFON (Mutual UFO Network) and the advent of the Freedom of Information Act, individuals began to demand greater accountability from the government regarding UFO phenomena. High-profile cases, including the Pentagon's acknowledgment of unidentified aerial phenomena (UAP) in the 2000s, reignited interest and debate over the existence of extraterrestrial life. These events serve as significant milestones in the discourse surrounding UFOs, illustrating a gradual shift from denial to a more open acknowledgment of the unknown. The government's increasing willingness to release classified documents has not only fueled public intrigue but has also provided fertile ground for the emergence of new religious movements centered around UFO beliefs.

The intersection of UFO disclosure and the rise of cults is particularly noteworthy in this historical context. The 1980s and 1990s saw a proliferation of UFO-related cults, such as Heaven's Gate and the Raelian movement, which capitalized on the public's anxieties and hopes regarding extraterrestrial life. These groups often framed their beliefs as revelations that transcended traditional religious doctrines, promoting a narrative that positioned aliens as saviors or superior beings. As government disclosures continued, these cults adapted their teachings to incorporate new information, suggesting a dynamic relationship between official narratives and the ideologies of such movements.

Social media has further transformed the landscape of UFO beliefs and their associated cults. The ability to share experiences and information instantaneously has spurred the formation of online communities that amplify belief in UFOs and extraterrestrial encounters. Platforms like YouTube, Facebook, and forums dedicated to UFO discussions have given rise to a new generation of influencers who shape public opinion and rally followers around specific narratives. This democratization of information dissemination has not only facilitated the spread of UFO-related beliefs but has also blurred the lines between credible research and sensationalist claims, complicating the psychological profiles of cult leaders who emerge in this digital age.

The historical context of UFO disclosure events underscores the intricate relationship between societal beliefs, governmental actions, and the formation of new religious movements. As public interest in extraterrestrial life continues to evolve, understanding the psychological underpinnings of cult leaders within this framework becomes essential. The dynamic nature of UFO beliefs, shaped by historical events and modern technology, poses ethical implications for contemporary society. The exploration of these themes reveals how UFO disclosure not only informs cultural narratives but also influences the spiritual landscapes of those drawn to the mysteries of the cosmos.

CULT FORMATION IN RESPONSE TO DISCLOSURE

Cult formation in response to disclosure often emerges as a complex interplay between societal anxieties, the allure of the unknown, and the fundamental human search for meaning. The phenomenon of UFO disclosure—whether through government revelations or public sightings—can create a fertile environment for new religious movements to take root. In this context, individuals seeking answers to existential questions may gravitate towards groups that provide a framework for understanding these experiences. The psychological need for belonging, coupled with a desire for knowledge about extraterrestrial life, often fuels the formation of cult-like communities that promise insights into both the cosmos and the self.

As UFO sightings gain media traction and governmental acknowledgment, the psychological dynamics influencing cult leaders become particularly significant. Many leaders capitalize on the uncertainty and fear surrounding disclosure to establish themselves as authoritative figures. By positioning themselves as intermediaries between the earthly realm and alien civilizations, these leaders exploit the ambiguity of the information presented to the public. This manipulation often entails crafting elaborate narratives that blend elements of science fiction with spiritual enlightenment, thereby attracting followers who seek clarity and hope in a rapidly changing world.

The role of social media in promoting UFO-related religious groups cannot be overstated. Platforms such as Facebook, Instagram, and YouTube facilitate the rapid dissemination of information, allowing cult leaders to reach a global audience. Online communities can foster a sense of belonging and validation among individuals who may feel isolated in their beliefs. Additionally, social media serves as a tool for cults to organize events, share testimonials, and create a shared identity among members. The ease of access to information and the ability to form connections online significantly contribute to the proliferation of these groups in response to disclosure events.

Historically, the formation of cults around alien encounters can be traced back to significant moments of revelation and uncertainty in society. Events such as the Roswell incident in 1947 or the Phoenix Lights in 1997 catalyzed the emergence of various organizations dedicated to exploring extraterrestrial phenomena. These historical touchpoints illustrate how collective experiences of witnessing the unexplainable can lead to the establishment of belief systems that challenge conventional religious and scientific paradigms. The psychological profiles of cult leaders during these pivotal moments reveal a pattern of charisma and manipulation, often rooted in their own encounters with the unknown.

The impact of government disclosure on cult membership trends highlights a cyclical relationship between authority, belief, and community. As official narratives around UFOs evolve, so too does the landscape of cults that draw upon these themes. Followers may experience a sense of urgency to align themselves with groups that interpret these disclosures in ways that resonate with their beliefs. This ongoing dialogue between governmental transparency and the spiritual interpretations offered by cult leaders underscores the ethical implications of such movements in contemporary society. The desire for truth, coupled with the allure of belonging, can create a precarious path that leads individuals into the arms of organizations that may prioritize ideology over individual well-being.

CASE STUDIES OF PROMINENT UFO CULTS

The emergence of UFO cults throughout the latter half of the twentieth century and into the twenty-first has often been a reflection of broader societal anxieties, technological advancements, and the search for meaning in an increasingly complex world. Prominent case studies reveal how charismatic leaders have harnessed the allure of extraterrestrial life to create compelling narratives that attract followers. One notable example is the Heaven's Gate cult, which gained notoriety in the 1990s. Led by Marshall Applewhite and Bonnie Nettles, the group proposed that Earth's imminent transformation would coincide with a spacecraft's arrival, promising ascension to a higher existence. Their tragic mass suicide in 1997 underscored the profound psychological grip such beliefs can exert on individuals seeking answers beyond conventional religious frameworks.

Another significant case is the Raelism movement, founded by Claude Vorilhon, who claims to have encountered extraterrestrial beings known as the Elohim. This cult emphasizes a doctrine of peace and scientific advancement, promoting the idea that humanity was created by these aliens through genetic engineering. Raelism stands out due to its attempts to engage with mainstream society through campaigns advocating for world peace, cloning, and the development of a new spiritual philosophy. Its leadership employs modern communication strategies, leveraging social media to extend its reach and influence, reflecting a growing trend among UFO-related groups to utilize contemporary platforms for recruitment and community building.

The Aetherius Society, established by George King in the 1950s, offers a different perspective on UFO beliefs. King claimed to receive messages from advanced extraterrestrial beings who sought to assist humanity in its spiritual evolution. The Society integrates elements of Eastern spirituality with UFO beliefs, advocating for a holistic approach to personal development and social responsibility. This case illustrates how traditional religious motifs can intertwine with UFO narratives, creating a unique blend that appeals to individuals disillusioned with conventional religious doctrines. The Society's rituals, which include prayer and meditation directed toward extraterrestrial beings, demonstrate the ritualistic practices often adopted by UFO cults to foster a sense of community and shared purpose among members.

The psychological profiles of these cult leaders reveal a complex interplay between personal charisma, visionary experiences, and the ability to manipulate followers' beliefs. Many leaders exhibit traits associated with narcissism and grandiosity, often positioning themselves as messianic figures destined to guide humanity through transformation. This phenomenon raises critical ethical implications regarding the responsibilities of such leaders and the potential for exploitation within these groups. As followers often seek belonging and clarity in their lives, the cult leader's role becomes pivotal in shaping their understanding of reality, underscoring the need for deeper examination of these dynamics within the context of UFO beliefs.

In conclusion, the case studies of prominent UFO cults highlight a significant intersection between contemporary spirituality and the allure of extraterrestrial life. These movements not only reflect individual psychological needs but also broader societal trends influenced by rapid technological changes and a quest for meaning. As UFO sightings continue to capture public imagination, the rise of new religious movements centered around these phenomena is likely to persist. Understanding the mechanisms behind these cults, from their leadership structures to their ritual practices, provides valuable insights into the evolving landscape of belief in the modern era, inviting further exploration of the ethical dimensions and societal impacts of such groups.

Chapter 3

Psychological Profiles of Cult Leaders

COMMON TRAITS OF CULT LEADERS

Cult leaders often share a set of common traits that facilitate their rise to power and the establishment of followings, particularly in the context of UFO beliefs and new religious movements. These traits often include charisma, a profound sense of purpose, and the ability to manipulate social dynamics within groups. Charisma is a crucial element; it allows leaders to inspire and captivate their followers, drawing them into a shared vision. This magnetic quality often masks underlying psychological manipulations and serves to solidify the leader's authority. Charismatic leaders can articulate complex ideas in simplified terms, making them accessible and appealing to a broad audience, particularly those searching for meaning in the often chaotic landscape of modern society.

Another prominent trait among cult leaders is the use of apocalyptic narratives that resonate with followers' fears and hopes. Many UFO-related cults thrive on the idea of impending transformation, whether through extraterrestrial intervention or catastrophic events. By positioning themselves as the bearers of critical knowledge or salvation, these leaders can instill a sense of urgency and exclusivity among their followers. This narrative often includes a promise of enlightenment or a new beginning, which can be particularly alluring to individuals disillusioned with traditional religious or societal structures. The apocalyptic framework not only bolsters group cohesion but also strengthens the leader's position as a gatekeeper of truth in a world perceived as increasingly chaotic.

Cult leaders also exhibit a penchant for creating an in-group versus out-group mentality. By fostering a sense of belonging and community, they isolate their followers from external influences and critical viewpoints. This division is often reinforced through rituals and practices that deepen the emotional bonds within the group while simultaneously demonizing outsiders or dissenters. In the context of UFO cults, this can manifest through the promotion of a shared identity rooted in unique beliefs about alien encounters or governmental conspiracies. As followers become more entrenched, they may develop an unwavering loyalty to the leader, viewing them as the sole source of truth about the universe and their place within it.

Psychological manipulation is another key characteristic of cult leaders. They often employ tactics such as love bombing, gaslighting, and emotional exploitation to maintain control over their followers. Love bombing, or overwhelming individuals with affection and attention, can create a dependency on the leader's approval. Gaslighting, on the other hand, erodes members' confidence in their own perceptions and experiences, making them more susceptible to the leader's interpretations of reality. This manipulation is particularly potent when combined with the promise of knowledge about extraterrestrial life and advanced technologies, which can enhance the leader's perceived authority.

Lastly, the adaptability of cult leaders is a significant trait that allows them to thrive in the rapidly evolving landscape of UFO beliefs. With the rise of social media and digital communication, these leaders can quickly disseminate their messages, engage with followers, and recruit new members. They often utilize modern technology to create a sense of immediacy and relevance, framing their ideas within contemporary discussions about science, spirituality, and conspiracy theories. This adaptability not only helps them maintain relevance but also allows them to respond to societal changes and capitalize on emerging trends, further entrenching their influence in the realm of UFO-related religious movements.

PSYCHOLOGICAL MANIPULATION TECHNIQUES

Psychological manipulation techniques employed by cult leaders often serve as critical tools in the establishment and maintenance of their influence over followers, particularly in movements centered around UFO beliefs. These techniques can vary widely, but they frequently include strategies such as love bombing, isolation, and the use of fear to control and shape the beliefs and behaviors of individuals. Cult leaders often create an environment that fosters dependency, making followers feel as though they cannot thrive outside the group. This dependency is often reinforced through a combination of emotional appeals and social pressure, effectively solidifying the leader's authority.

One prominent technique is love bombing, where cult leaders shower potential recruits with affection and attention to create a sense of belonging and acceptance. This initial phase often targets vulnerable individuals who may be seeking community or validation. By establishing a strong emotional connection, leaders can easily guide followers into deeper commitments to the group. In the context of UFO cults, this technique is particularly potent, as it aligns with the promise of profound knowledge about extraterrestrial life and the universe, further enticing individuals to invest their time and energy in the group's activities.

Isolation is another critical method used to control members. Cult leaders often encourage followers to distance themselves from friends, family, and other outside influences that challenge the group's ideology.

This physical and emotional separation creates an echo chamber where only the cult's beliefs are validated and reinforced. In UFO-related movements, such isolation can lead to a heightened sense of urgency and importance surrounding the group's narrative, as members become increasingly reliant on one another for affirmation of their beliefs. The absence of external perspectives further solidifies the cult s worldview, making it challenging for members to question or leave the group.

Fear tactics also play a significant role in psychological manipulation within UFO cults. Leaders may propagate apocalyptic scenarios or dire consequences for those who do not adhere to the group's teachings. By instilling a sense of fear regarding the repercussions of non-compliance, leaders can maintain control over their followers. This is particularly effective in UFO cults, where narratives often include themes of cosmic judgment or impending alien intervention. Such fear not only keeps members compliant but also deepens their commitment to the group, as they perceive their allegiance as essential for their safety and salvation.

Finally, the use of cognitive dissonance is a powerful psychological tool employed by cult leaders. When followers encounter information that contradicts the cult's teachings, leaders may employ various strategies to mitigate the discomfort associated with this dissonance. This may involve redefining the beliefs, dismissing opposing views as misinformation, or reinforcing the idea that only the group possesses the truth about alien encounters. By systematically addressing cognitive dissonance, cult leaders effectively safeguard their influence and encourage unwavering loyalty among followers, thereby perpetuating the cycle of belief and commitment that characterizes UFO cults.

THE ROLE OF CHARISMA IN LEADERSHIP

Charisma plays a pivotal role in the landscape of leadership, particularly within the context of cults that have emerged around UFO beliefs. Leaders of these groups often possess a magnetic charm that draws individuals towards them, creating a sense of connection and trust. This quality not only facilitates the formation of a devoted following but also allows leaders to articulate complex ideas related to extraterrestrial life and spiritual enlightenment in a manner that resonates deeply with their audience. The ability to inspire and motivate followers through compelling narratives about UFOs and alien encounters is a hallmark of charismatic leadership, enabling these figures to cultivate a strong sense of community among believers.

One of the key psychological mechanisms by which charisma operates is the creation of an idealized vision of reality. Cult leaders often present themselves as possessors of unique knowledge about extraterrestrial beings and their intentions towards humanity. This perceived wisdom, coupled with a dynamic personality, can lead followers to feel as though they are part of something greater than themselves. In the realm of UFO-based religions, this idealization can manifest through the portrayal of an impending transformation or ascension, which is framed as achievable only through adherence to the leader's teachings. Such beliefs can be particularly appealing in times of social uncertainty, where individuals seek meaning and direction.

The intersection of charisma and authority becomes increasingly complex in the age of social media. Platforms such as YouTube, Instagram, and Facebook have facilitated the rapid dissemination of charismatic leadership styles, allowing cult leaders to reach wider audiences than ever before. These leaders often utilize persuasive techniques, such as emotional storytelling and visual imagery, to captivate their followers. By creating an online persona that embodies charisma, they can engage with both existing members and potential recruits, blurring the lines between personal interaction and digital presence. This phenomenon has significant implications for the growth and sustainability of UFO-related religious movements.

Moreover, the psychological profile of charismatic leaders often reveals a blend of traits that enhance their effectiveness. Many exhibit high levels of self-confidence, sociability, and emotional expressiveness, which can enhance their appeal. Their ability to read social cues and respond empathetically contributes to the development of strong interpersonal connections with followers. This responsiveness fosters an environment where individuals feel understood and valued, reinforcing their commitment to the group and its beliefs. In a milieu where traditional societal structures may feel inadequate, such leaders offer an alternative source of validation and belonging.

Lastly, the ethical implications of charismatic leadership in the context of UFO cults cannot be overlooked. While charisma can inspire positive change and foster community, it can also lead to manipulation and exploitation. The intense loyalty that charismatic figures can inspire may result in followers making significant personal sacrifices, sometimes to the detriment of their well-being. As the phenomenon of UFO cults continues to evolve, it is crucial for researchers and enthusiasts alike to critically examine the role of charisma in these dynamics, understanding both its potential to uplift and its capacity to control. Through this lens, a deeper understanding of the psychological forces at play within these movements can be achieved, enriching the discourse surrounding UFO beliefs and their societal impact.

Chapter 4

Influence of UFOs on New Religious Movements

ANALYSIS OF KEY UFO SIGHTINGS AND THEIR IMPACT

The analysis of key UFO sightings reveals a complex interplay between societal beliefs and the emergence of new religious movements. Notable incidents, such as the 1947

Roswell crash and the 1973 Pascagoula abduction, catalyzed a growing fascination with extraterrestrial life, which in turn fostered the formation of various cults and spiritual groups. These sightings often serve as foundational narratives for these movements, providing not only a framework for belief but also a sense of community among adherents who find solace in shared experiences of the unexplained. The psychological impact of these sightings is profound, as they tap into deep-seated fears and hopes regarding humanity's place in the universe.

The influence of UFO sightings extends beyond mere anecdotal evidence; they reshape cultural landscapes and influence individual worldviews. For instance, the rise of the Heaven's Gate cult in the 1990s illustrates how prominent sightings can be interpreted as divine messages. Followers adopt these narratives, often restructuring their lives around the belief that they are chosen for a higher purpose. This phenomenon is not limited to one group; various other cults have similarly emerged, reflecting a broader trend where UFO sightings serve as pivotal events that guide the formation of new belief systems. The psychological profiles of cult leaders often reveal a charismatic ability to reinterpret these sightings, presenting them as harbingers of a new spiritual era.

Moreover, the historical analysis of cults formed around alien encounters demonstrates that UFO sightings often coincide with periods of societal upheaval or technological advancement. The Cold War era, for example, led to increased anxiety about existential threats, which many interpreted through the lens of extraterrestrial encounters. This historical context not only legitimizes the experiences reported by followers but also reinforces the leaders' narratives, allowing them to maintain authority and control over their members. The cyclical nature of these sightings and the ensuing cult formations suggest a persistent human need to find meaning in chaos, often leading to the establishment of rigid belief systems that can resist critical scrutiny.

In recent years, social media has played a crucial role in promoting UFO-related religious groups. Platforms that facilitate discussion and dissemination of information have enabled these movements to reach wider audiences, often resulting in rapid growth. Personal testimonies shared online can validate experiences and encourage new members to join, creating a feedback loop of belief reinforcement. The accessibility of information also allows for the blending of traditional religious motifs with contemporary UFO beliefs, leading to innovative spiritual practices that attract diverse followers. This phenomenon highlights the adaptability of cults in the digital age, where the immediacy of communication can amplify both the allure of UFO sightings and the fervor of belief.

The impact of government disclosure on cult membership trends is another area of interest. As official acknowledgments of UFO phenomena increase, they lend a sense of legitimacy to the beliefs espoused by these groups. Many cults have harnessed this newfound openness to attract disillusioned individuals seeking answers in an age of uncertainty. Consequently, the intersection of UFO beliefs and mainstream discourse is shifting, challenging traditional boundaries between science, spirituality, and societal norms. The ethical implications of this dynamic are significant, as it raises questions about the responsibilities of leaders in guiding their followers and the potential consequences of such beliefs in an increasingly complex world.

FORMATION OF BELIEFS AROUND SIGHTINGS

The formation of beliefs around UFO sightings represents a complex interplay of individual psychology, social dynamics, and cultural narratives. As sightings proliferate, they often serve as catalysts for broader belief systems that transcend mere fascination with extraterrestrial life. These events can trigger profound personal and collective experiences, leading individuals to interpret unexplained phenomena through the lens of spirituality, community, and existential inquiry. The specific ways in which these beliefs solidify can be traced through historical patterns of new religious movements that emerge in tandem with waves of reported sightings.

Psychological profiles of cult leaders reveal a distinct pattern whereby charismatic individuals harness the collective anxiety and curiosity surrounding UFO phenomena. These leaders often capitalize on the ambiguity of sightings, framing them as divine messages or signs of an impending transformation. By weaving together narratives that emphasize alien contact as a means of achieving enlightenment or salvation, they attract followers seeking answers to life's fundamental questions. The emotional appeal of these beliefs is heightened by the leader's ability to create a sense of belonging and purpose, thereby solidifying the group's commitment to the ideology.

The influence of social media in shaping these beliefs cannot be understated. Platforms such as Facebook, Twitter, and YouTube serve as fertile ground for the spread of UFO-related content, allowing for the rapid dissemination of sightings, theories, and testimonies. This democratization of information enables individuals to connect with like-minded enthusiasts, fostering communities that may further entrench belief systems around sightings. The viral nature of such content often amplifies existing anxieties about government secrecy and the unknown, driving a wedge between mainstream perspectives and the emerging narratives espoused by UFO-focused groups.

Historically, the intersection of UFO sightings with cult formation reveals a cyclical pattern. Each major wave of reported sightings often coincides with the rise of new religious movements that reinterpret these events in ways consistent with their doctrines. As believers engage with the narratives promoted by these movements, they often adopt rituals and practices that reinforce their beliefs, drawing parallels to traditional religious frameworks. This blending of the sacred and the speculative allows for a rich tapestry of spiritual expression that appeals to individuals disillusioned with conventional religious structures.

As the conversation surrounding government disclosure of UFO-related information continues to evolve, the implications for cult membership trends are significant. Increased transparency may lead to a re-evaluation of beliefs held by existing members while simultaneously attracting new adherents drawn by the promise of unveiled truths. Ethical considerations emerge as these movements navigate the fine line between legitimate inquiry and exploitation of vulnerable individuals seeking meaning. Understanding the formation of beliefs around sightings is crucial for comprehending the broader sociocultural dynamics at play in the modern landscape of UFO-related religions.

NEW RELIGIOUS MOVEMENTS: CASE STUDIES

New religious movements (NRMs) often emerge in response to profound societal changes, and the era of UFO beliefs is no exception. In recent decades, various groups have formed around the premise of extraterrestrial life and its significance to human existence. These movements typically blend elements of spirituality, science fiction, and apocalyptic thinking, creating a unique psychological landscape that attracts individuals seeking meaning and community. Case studies of notable NRMs, such as Heaven's Gate and the Raelian Movement, illustrate how beliefs in UFOs and alien encounters can catalyze new religious ideologies.

Heaven's Gate, perhaps one of the most infamous NRMs, was founded by Marshall Applewhite and Bonnie Nettles in the 1970s. This group combined Christian theology with beliefs about extraterrestrial beings, positing that the Earth was transitioning to a higher level of existence. Members were encouraged to prepare for their ascension by severing ties with the material world, culminating in the tragic mass suicide in 1997. The psychological profile of Applewhite reveals a complex interplay of charisma, delusion, and a deep sense of purpose that resonated with followers, illustrating how a strong leader can mobilize individuals around a shared belief in UFOs as harbingers of spiritual transformation.

The Raelian Movement offers a contrasting case study, founded by Claude Vorilhon, who claims to have met extraterrestrial beings called the Elohim. This movement emphasizes a more optimistic view of alien contact, focusing on themes of peace, love, and scientific advancement. Raelians actively promote the idea of human cloning as a means to achieve immortality, intertwining their spiritual beliefs with contemporary scientific discourse. The movement's use of social media has allowed it to reach a broader audience, demonstrating how digital platforms facilitate the spread of UFO-related religious ideologies and attract diverse members seeking alternative spiritual paths.

In examining the historical context of NRMs centered on UFO beliefs, it is crucial to consider the impact of government disclosure on membership trends. As official narratives about unidentified aerial phenomena (UAP) gain traction, individuals may become more open to exploring spiritual interpretations of these experiences. The psychological implications of such disclosures can lead to an increase in cult membership, as adherents may interpret government acknowledgment of UAPs as validation of their beliefs. This phenomenon underscores the dynamic relationship between societal events and the formation of new religious movements.

The rituals and practices of UFO-based religions often reflect a blend of traditional religious elements and modern spiritual themes. These may include communal gatherings, meditation sessions, and elaborate ceremonies that seek to connect members with extraterrestrial entities. The intersection of science fiction and modern spirituality is evident in these practices, as members engage with narratives that challenge conventional understandings of existence. Personal testimonies from former cult members reveal the profound influence of these rituals on their beliefs and identities, raising ethical questions about the psychological manipulation that can occur within such groups. The exploration of these case studies highlights the complex interplay between belief, leadership, and the broader cultural context surrounding UFO phenomena.

Chapter 5

Historical Analysis of Cults Formed Around Aliens

EARLY 20TH CENTURY CULTS AND UFOS

Early 20th century America witnessed a significant rise in the formation of cults, many of which revolved around the burgeoning fascination with UFOs and extraterrestrial life. The social and cultural landscape of the time was marked by technological advancements and a growing public interest in space exploration. This environment created fertile ground for new religious movements that sought to incorporate scientific discoveries into spiritual frameworks. Groups such as the Theosophical Society and later, the Raëlian Movement, emerged during this period, intertwining elements of mysticism with the allure of alien encounters and advanced civilizations, thereby shaping a new narrative that appealed to many disillusioned with traditional religious institutions.

The influence of UFO sightings on these new religious movements cannot be overstated. The 1947 Roswell incident, coupled with a series of high-profile sightings, ignited public imagination and curiosity about extraterrestrial life. These events were often interpreted through a spiritual lens, leading many to perceive UFOs not merely as physical phenomena but as signs from higher beings. Cult leaders adeptly harnessed this societal intrigue, often presenting themselves as mediators between humanity and these advanced extraterrestrial intelligences. Their claims frequently included prophecies or messages from alien civilizations, which provided followers with a sense of purpose and belonging in an increasingly complex world.

Psychological profiles of cult leaders during this era reveal a pattern of charismatic authority combined with a deep understanding of their followers' vulnerabilities. Many leaders, such as George Adamski and Marshall Applewhite, effectively tapped into societal fears, hopes, and aspirations, using alien narratives to create a compelling vision of salvation or enlightenment. By positioning themselves as chosen channels of communication with extraterrestrial entities, these leaders exploited the psychological needs of individuals seeking community and answers to existential questions. This dynamic not only solidified their control but also fostered an environment where critical thinking was often suppressed in favor of blind faith.

Historical analysis of cults formed around alien encounters indicates that these movements often served as a reaction to broader social anxieties, including technological change, war, and the potential for global catastrophe. The early 20th century was marked by significant upheaval, including both World Wars and the Great Depression, leading individuals to search for alternative belief systems that could offer hope and stability. As traditional religious frameworks seemed inadequate to address the realities of modern life, UFO cults emerged as appealing alternatives that promised not only answers but also a sense of cosmic destiny. This intersection of culture, fear, and belief facilitated the evolution of a unique spiritual landscape that continues to influence contemporary society.

The role of social media in promoting UFO-related religious groups has further transformed the dynamics established in the early 20th century. Today, the proliferation of digital platforms allows for instantaneous communication and the rapid spread of ideas. This environment mirrors the early 20th-century fascination with UFOs and cults, where charismatic leaders could utilize technology to amplify their messages. Social media enables followers to connect, share experiences, and validate beliefs in ways that were previously unimaginable, thereby creating virtual communities that can rival those of traditional religious organizations. As these groups continue to evolve, their impact on societal values and individual psychology remains a critical area for ongoing research and exploration.

THE 1960S AND 1970S: A CULT EXPLOSION

The 1960s and 1970s marked a significant period in the evolution of new religious movements, particularly those centered around UFO beliefs and extraterrestrial encounters. This era witnessed a surge in the number of cults that not only embraced the concept of alien life but also positioned themselves as conduits for messages from these otherworldly beings. The backdrop of the Cold War, coupled with increasing societal unrest and a quest for alternative spiritualities, created a fertile ground for the emergence and proliferation of these groups. As traditional religious frameworks began to wane in influence, many individuals turned to the idea of UFOs as a means of exploring existential questions and seeking community.

A notable aspect of this cult explosion was the psychological profile of the leaders who emerged during this time. Many of these figures possessed charismatic traits that allowed them to attract followers who were often disillusioned with conventional beliefs. They capitalized on the zeitgeist of the era, utilizing media coverage of UFO sightings and government investigations, such as Project Blue Book, to validate their claims. These leaders frequently presented themselves as

enlightened beings or messengers of extraterrestrial intelligences, offering their followers a sense of purpose and belonging in
an increasingly chaotic world.

The influence of UFO sightings on the formation of these new religions cannot be overstated. High-profile events, such as the
Roswell incident and the Betty and Barney
Hill abduction case, galvanized public interest and provided a narrative framework for
cult leaders to build upon. These incidents
served as touchstones for many believers,
fostering a collective identity that transcended individual experiences. As reports of
alien encounters gained traction in popular
culture, they were woven into the fabric of
the cults' teachings, reinforcing the notion
that humanity was not alone and that salvation could be found through communion
with extraterrestrial beings.

Social media, although not as prominent
in the 1960s and 1970s as it is today, played
a nascent role in connecting like-minded individuals. Early forms of communication,

such as newsletters and small press publications, allowed leaders to disseminate their beliefs and rally followers. As technology evolved, these groups began to utilize radio and television appearances to broaden their reach and influence. The proliferation of these channels enabled the rapid sharing of information, creating echo chambers where individuals could reinforce their beliefs about UFOs and their associated cults.

The intersection of science fiction and spirituality during this period also merits analysis. The cultural fascination with space exploration, fueled by the space race, infused many cult ideologies with elements borrowed from popular science fiction narratives. Leaders often appropriated themes from literature and film to craft compelling mythologies that resonated with their followers. This blending of genres not only legitimized their beliefs but also appealed to a demographic hungry for alternative explanations about existence and the universe. In retrospect, the cult explosion of the 1960s and 1970s represents a pivotal moment in the ongoing dialogue between human spirituality and the enigmatic allure of the cosmos.

MODERN CULTS AND ALIEN ENCOUNTERS

Modern cults centered around alien encounters often emerge within a unique cultural landscape shaped by the increasing fascination with UFO phenomena. This phenomenon can be traced back to the mid-20th century, when reports of unidentified flying objects began to proliferate. As these sightings captured public imagination, they paved the way for new religious movements that integrated extraterrestrial beliefs into their doctrines. Cult leaders adept at capitalizing on this intrigue often construct narratives that position themselves as intermediaries between humanity and otherworldly beings, fostering a sense of purpose and community among followers who share a profound curiosity about the cosmos.

Psychologically, the appeal of these cults can be analyzed through the lens of existential anxiety and the search for meaning. In an era marked by rapid technological advancements and societal upheaval, individuals may turn to the certainty offered by cult leaders who claim to possess exclusive knowledge about alien life and its implications for humanity. This dynamic creates a fertile environment for the formation of cults, where charismatic leaders leverage their authority to provide answers to existential questions. The psychological profiles of these leaders often reveal traits such as narcissism, grandiosity, and a deep-seated need for control, which resonate with followers who seek clarity in an increasingly complex world.

The role of social media in promoting UFO-related religious groups cannot be overstated. Platforms such as Facebook, Instagram, and YouTube serve as crucial tools for these movements to disseminate their beliefs and attract new members. The viral nature of online content allows for rapid spread of ideologies, making it easier for cults to reach a global audience. Social media also fosters a sense of belonging among members, as they can connect with like-minded individuals and share personal testimonies that reinforce their shared beliefs. This digital landscape has transformed traditional recruitment methods, making it possible for cults to thrive in an age where geographical boundaries are less relevant.

Historically, the intersection of traditional religions and UFO cults reveals a complex tapestry of belief systems that borrow elements from one another. Many modern cults adopt rituals reminiscent of established religious practices, such as communal gatherings, symbolic ceremonies, and the use of sacred texts. This syncretism often serves to legitimize the extraterrestrial narrative while providing followers with familiar frameworks for understanding their experiences. By analyzing these commonalities, researchers can gain insights into how contemporary spirituality evolves in response to modern challenges, as well as the underlying psychological mechanisms that sustain these belief systems.

The impact of government disclosure on cult membership trends presents another critical area of study. As official acknowledgment of UFOs becomes more prevalent, the narratives constructed by cult leaders may shift to incorporate new information, thereby maintaining relevance in the eyes of followers. This evolution can lead to fluctuations in membership, as individuals may feel a renewed sense of urgency to seek answers from these groups. Furthermore, as discussions around ethics and the implications of such beliefs gain traction, researchers must consider the broader societal consequences of UFO cults, particularly regarding mental health, community cohesion, and the potential for exploitation of vulnerable individuals seeking answers in an uncertain world.

Chapter 6

Role of Social Media in UFO-Related Religion

SOCIAL MEDIA PLATFORMS AND CULT OUTREACH

Social media platforms have become a vital tool for the outreach of cults, particularly those centered around UFO beliefs and encounters. These platforms provide a unique environment for the rapid dissemination of information, allowing leaders to connect with potential followers across vast geographical distances. In the context of UFO-related cults, social media serves not only as a means of communication but also as a space for building community, sharing experiences, and fostering a sense of belonging among individuals who may feel marginalized or misunderstood in mainstream society. The interactive nature of these platforms enables leaders to engage with their audience, creating a dynamic that strengthens the appeal of their ideologies and practices.

The influence of social media extends beyond mere communication; it plays a crucial role in shaping the narratives that surround UFO phenomena. Cult leaders utilize platforms such as Facebook, Twitter, and Instagram to curate content that aligns with their beliefs, often amplifying sensational stories of alien encounters or government conspiracies. This curation helps to establish a compelling narrative that not only attracts new members but also reinforces the loyalty of existing followers. The accessibility of visual media, including videos and memes, further enhances the persuasive power of these narratives, making them more relatable and engaging for a digital audience.

Moreover, social media facilitates the formation of echo chambers where like-minded individuals can reinforce their beliefs. This phenomenon is particularly prevalent in the realm of UFO cults, where members often share personal testimonies and experiences that validate the group's ideology. As followers interact with one another, they create a shared reality that is insulated from external critiques. This communal reinforcement can lead to a heightened sense of urgency and conviction regarding their beliefs, often resulting in increased commitment to the group. The psychological effects of such environments can be profound, as individuals may find solace and affirmation in the collective experience of perceived alien encounters.

The rise of these digital communities has also transformed the recruitment strategies employed by UFO cults. Traditional methods of outreach, such as in-person meetings or pamphlet distribution, have largely been supplanted by online engagement strategies that prioritize accessibility and immediacy. Cult leaders often employ targeted advertising and algorithm-driven content to reach individuals who have shown interest in related topics, thus ensuring that their messages resonate with potential recruits. The ability to analyze engagement metrics allows leaders to fine-tune their approaches, making their outreach efforts more effective than ever before.

Finally, the impact of social media on the dynamics of UFO cults raises important ethical considerations. While these platforms can empower individuals to explore alternative beliefs and find community, they also pose risks of manipulation and exploitation by charismatic leaders. The rapid spread of misinformation can create environments ripe for psychological distress, particularly among those seeking answers to existential questions. As disclosure enthusiasts and researchers examine the intersection of social media and UFO cults, it is crucial to consider both the potential for connection and the dangers of unchecked influence, striving for a nuanced understanding of this complex landscape.

THE IMPACT OF ONLINE COMMUNITIES

The emergence of online communities has significantly transformed the landscape of UFO beliefs and the subsequent rise of cults and new religious movements. These digital spaces serve as platforms for individuals who share a fascination with extraterrestrial life, offering a sense of belonging and validation that may be lacking in their offline lives. Within these forums and social media groups, members exchange personal experiences, theories and insights about UFO sightings and alien encounters. This collective engagement enhances the appeal of

UFO-related narratives and can lead to the formation of tightly-knit communities that often blur the lines between fandom and spiritual belief.

The influence of online communities on the formation of new religious movements centered around UFO beliefs cannot be over-stated. These platforms allow for the rapid dissemination of information, enabling charismatic leaders to reach wider audiences than ever before. Cult leaders leverage the anonymity and accessibility of the internet to promote their ideologies, often framing their messages in ways that resonate with contemporary societal anxieties and desires for connection. The ability to connect with like-minded individuals fosters a shared iden-tity, which can be crucial in solidifying the cult's appeal and attracting new members who are searching for meaning or answers to existential questions.

Additionally, the psychological profiles of cult leaders often reflect a keen understand-ing of online dynamics. Many leaders exhibit traits of narcissism or grandiosity, capitalizing on their followers' emotional vulnerabilities. They may use social media to craft an idealized image of themselves, presenting themselves as enlightened beings with exclusive knowledge about extraterrestrial life and the universe. This manipulation of online personas can create a power dynamic that reinforces their authority and further entrenches members in the community's beliefs, making it increasingly difficult for individuals to question or leave the group.

Historically, cults formed around alien encounters have evolved alongside technological advancements, and the internet has accelerated this evolution. Unlike previous generations that relied on in-person gatherings and printed materials, contemporary groups can maintain continuous engagement through live streams, podcasts, and interactive content. This constant exposure solidifies belief systems and rituals, creating an environment where skepticism is often met with hostility. The rituals and practices of

UFO-based religions are thus informed by an online culture that prizes immediacy and emotional resonance over critical analysis, leading to an atmosphere where dogma can flourish unchecked.

The implications of these online communities extend beyond personal belief systems; they raise ethical questions regarding the responsibility of platform providers and the potential for manipulation. As governments and organizations engage in disclosure about UFO phenomena, the role of these communities in shaping public perception and belief becomes increasingly critical. Understanding the dynamics at play within these digital spheres can provide insight into how cults adapt and evolve in response to new information, ultimately contributing to a broader understanding of contemporary spirituality and the cultural significance of UFO beliefs. The intersection of technology, psychology, and spirituality in this context necessitates ongoing examination and critical discourse, particularly as we navigate the implications for both individuals and society at large.

CASE STUDIES OF SOCIAL MEDIA SUCCESS STORIES

In the evolving landscape of UFO beliefs and the emergence of new religious movements, social media has emerged as a powerful tool for cult leaders seeking to attract and retain followers. Numerous case studies illustrate how specific individuals and groups have harnessed platforms like Facebook, Twitter, and YouTube to create a sense of community and urgency around their extraterrestrial narratives. One notable example is the case of the "Heaven's Gate" group, which successfully utilized early internet forums to disseminate their beliefs about ascension and alien contact. Their online presence allowed them to connect with like-minded individuals who were seeking answers to existential questions, ultimately fostering a devoted following.

Another compelling case study is that of the "Rael Movement," which has leveraged social media to spread its message of extraterrestrial contact and human evolution. Through a combination of engaging content, personal testimonials, and strategic use of hashtags, the Rael Movement has cultivated a global community that fervently believes in their teachings. The movement's leaders have effectively employed social media to create a narrative that positions them as conduits of important revelations about humanity's origins and its future, drawing in individuals who feel disenfranchised by mainstream religions.

Additionally, the rise of platforms like YouTube has allowed for the proliferation of UFO-related documentaries and personal accounts that resonate deeply with audiences. Channels dedicated to UFO sightings, alien encounters, and related conspiracy theories have amassed millions of subscribers, creating a rich environment for cult leaders to exploit. For instance, the "Disclosure Movement," which advocates for transparency regarding governmental knowledge of extraterrestrial life, has seen significant growth through viral videos and live streams that engage viewers emotionally. This phenomenon illustrates how compelling visual content can amplify messages and foster a sense of belonging among those who share similar beliefs.

The case of the "Church of the SubGenius" further highlights the intersection of humor, satire, and serious belief systems in the age of social media. By combining absurdity with genuine spiritual messages, this group has attracted a diverse following that thrives on the playful critique of traditional religious structures. Their social media campaigns often blur the lines between parody and genuine belief, appealing to a demographic that values both entertainment and a sense of community in their quest for understanding the cosmos.

Finally, the impact of government disclosure on UFO-related cults cannot be overstated. As official acknowledgment of unidentified aerial phenomena (UAP) becomes more frequent, groups like the "Galactic Federation" have capitalized on this momentum. Their social media strategies include real-time updates and interpretations of governmental announcements, creating a sense of urgency and relevance around their teachings. This responsiveness not only keeps followers engaged but also positions the leaders as authoritative figures in a rapidly changing discourse, demonstrating how adeptly they navigate the contemporary landscape of belief and skepticism surrounding UFOs.

Chapter 7

Compare Traditional Religions and UFO Cult Belief

SIMILARITIES BETWEEN UFO CULTS AND TRADITIONAL RELIGIONS

UFO cults and traditional religions exhibit a striking array of similarities that warrant a detailed examination. Both structures often revolve around a central figure or doctrine that serves as a focal point for believers. In traditional religions, this may be a prophet, deity, or sacred text, while in UFO cults, it often manifests in the form of charismatic leaders or specific extraterrestrial beings. These figures or entities provide a framework for understanding the universe, offering adherents a sense of purpose and belonging. The narratives constructed around these leaders or beings often fulfill fundamental human needs for meaning, community, and transcendence.

Ritualistic practices are another common thread linking UFO cults and traditional religions. Both groups engage in ceremonies that are intended to reinforce beliefs and foster a sense of connection among members. In traditional religions, these rituals can range from weekly worship services to annual festivals, while UFO cults may hold meetings, group meditations, or even elaborate events designed to invoke contact with extraterrestrial entities. These rituals not only serve to strengthen group identity but also create an environment that validates personal experiences of the extraordinary, whether those experiences are rooted in divine encounters or alleged alien abductions.

The concept of salvation or transcendence is prevalent in both UFO cults and traditional religions. Adherents of traditional faiths often seek salvation in the form of an afterlife or spiritual enlightenment, while UFO cults frequently promise a form of ascension or transformation, often tied to future events such as alien interventions or apocalyptic scenarios. This promise of a better existence—be it in a heavenly realm or through an extraterrestrial evolution—serves as a powerful motivating factor for followers, reinforcing their commitment to the belief system and its leader. Such narratives can also provide a coping mechanism for individuals facing existential anxieties in a rapidly changing world.

Community and social identity play crucial roles in both UFO cults and traditional religions. Members often find in these groups a sense of belonging that may be lacking in their everyday lives. This communal aspect is vital for the reinforcement of beliefs and the maintenance of group cohesion. Traditional religions often have well-established social structures and support networks, while UFO cults may create their own unique social dynamics, often characterized by intense loyalty to the group and its tenets. The shared experience of UFO sightings or encounters can deepen bonds among members, akin to the fellowship found in traditional religious congregations.

Finally, the use of narratives and mythologies serves as a bridge between UFO cults and traditional religions. Both rely on storytelling to convey fundamental truths and to articulate the beliefs that define their identities. This shared narrative function allows for the interpretation of both historical events and personal experiences through a lens that emphasizes the extraordinary. In traditional religions, sacred stories often convey moral lessons and community values; in UFO cults, tales of alien encounters, prophecies, and the promise of contact provide frameworks for understanding the unknown. These narratives not only shape individual belief systems but also influence broader cultural perceptions of the supernatural, further intertwining the realms of UFO beliefs and traditional religious thought.

DIFFERENCES IN DOCTRINE AND PRACTICE

The differences in doctrine and practice among UFO-related cults highlight the diverse interpretations of extraterrestrial encounters and their implications for humanity. Many of these groups emerge from a blend of traditional spiritual beliefs and modern UFO sightings, resulting in unique belief systems that often diverge significantly from mainstream religions. For instance, some cults may adopt a Gnostic framework, viewing extraterrestrials as enlightened beings who offer secret knowledge necessary for spiritual ascension, while others may focus on apocalyptic narratives, positioning aliens as either saviors or harbingers of doom. This divergence reflects not only the theological diversity within these movements but also the varying psychological needs of their followers, who seek answers to existential questions that contemporary society often fails to address.

In practice, the rituals and community activities of UFO cults can vary widely, shaped by their distinct doctrinal beliefs. Some cults emphasize communal gatherings where members share personal experiences of alien contact, reinforcing group identity and collective belief. Others may adopt more structured practices, such as meditation, channeling extraterrestrial messages, or engaging in elaborate ceremonies designed to invoke contact with alien beings. The integration of technology, particularly social media, has also transformed these practices;

online platforms serve as spaces for recruitment, dissemination of beliefs, and virtual rituals, allowing groups to expand their influence beyond geographical limitations. This technological adaptation illustrates how contemporary UFC cults navigate the modern landscape while maintaining their distinct religious practices.

Moreover, the psychological profiles of cult leaders play a crucial role in shaping both doctrine and practice within these movements. Charismatic leaders often emerge as central figures, claiming special knowledge or direct communication with extraterrestrial entities. Their authority is frequently reinforced through personal testimonies about encounters, which serve to validate their leadership and attract followers. Understanding these leaders' psychological motivations—ranging from a desire for power to genuine belief in their messages—can provide insights into the dynamics of belief formation within UFO cults. This dynamic between leader and followers is critical in fostering adherence to the group's doctrines and practices, as the psychological dependency on the leader can lead to an intense commitment to the cult's ideology.

The historical context of UFO cults also reveals how societal factors influence their development. The advent of the space age, combined with key cultural moments such as the Roswell incident and the popularity of science fiction, has catalyzed the formation of new religious movements around UFO beliefs. These historical events are often woven into the narratives of cults, providing a framework for their doctrines that resonates with contemporary anxieties regarding technology, authority, and the unknown. The intersection of historical events with personal experiences of alien encounters further enriches the belief systems of these groups, making their doctrines not only a reflection of individual psychology but also a response to broader societal narratives.

Finally, the ethical implications of these differences in doctrine and practice cannot be overlooked. The rise of UFO cults raises questions about manipulation, consent, and the psychological well-being of members. The varying degrees of vulnerability among followers can lead to exploitative dynamics, particularly in groups where leaders may prioritize personal gain over the welfare of their members. As researchers and enthusiasts examine these movements, it is essential to consider the ethical dimensions of their practices and the potential impact on individuals seeking connection, understanding, and meaning in an increasingly complex world. By analyzing the differences in doctrine and practice, one can better comprehend the allure of these cults and the profound psychological and social factors at play in the realm of UFO beliefs.

THE EVOLVING NATURE OF BELIEF SYSTEMS

The landscape of belief systems has undergone significant transformation, particularly in the context of UFO-related movements. As the phenomenon of unidentified flying objects captures public imagination, new religious movements emerge, often characterized by a blend of spiritual and extraterrestrial themes. This evolving nature of belief systems reflects not only the changing societal attitudes towards science and spirituality but also the psychological needs of individuals seeking meaning in an increasingly complex world. The intersection of these factors has facilitated the rise of cults that orbit around the allure of alien encounters, promising insights into humanity's place in the cosmos.

Historically, belief systems have adapted to the prevailing cultural narratives, and the UFO phenomenon is no exception. The post-World War II era marked a significant turning point, where the combination of technological advancements, space exploration, and the Cold War climate contributed to a fertile ground for new ideologies. Cult leaders have emerged as pivotal figures in this paradigm shift, often capitalizing on the fears and hopes of their followers. By presenting themselves as intermediaries between the human experience and extraterrestrial intelligence, these leaders redefine spiritual authority, drawing parallels to traditional religious figures while operating within a distinctly modern framework.

The influence of social media has further accelerated the evolution of belief systems surrounding UFOs. Platforms that facilitate the rapid dissemination of information allow for the formation of communities that may not have existed previously. These online spaces enable individuals to share experiences, validate beliefs, and engage with like-minded others, thus reinforcing their commitment to UFO-centric ideologies. As a result, social media serves not only as a communication tool but also as a catalyst for the creation and sustenance of new religious movements, blurring the lines between traditional religious practices and contemporary spiritual expressions.

Moreover, the psychological profiles of cult leaders reveal a complex interplay of charisma, authority, and manipulation. Many leaders exhibit traits that resonate with followers' desires for belonging and understanding in a chaotic world. By constructing narratives that intertwine personal experiences with broader cosmic themes, these leaders can maintain a grip on their followers, guiding them through rituals and practices that reinforce group identity. This dynamic becomes particularly pronounced in the context of emerging belief systems, where the promise of alien contact often serves as a metaphor for deeper existential quests.

As government disclosure initiatives gain momentum, the implications for cult membership trends become increasingly evident. The normalization of UFO discourse may attract new adherents while simultaneously challenging the narratives of established groups. This evolving landscape raises critical ethical questions regarding the responsibility of leaders and the psychological impact on members. Understanding these dynamics is crucial for researchers and enthusiasts alike, as it sheds light on the broader implications of belief systems in the context of human psychology and societal change, ultimately enriching the discourse surrounding alien messiahs and their followers.

Chapter 8

The Intersection of SciFi and Modern Spirituality

INFLUENCE OF SCIENCE FICTION ON UFO BELIEFS

The intersection of science fiction and UFO beliefs has significantly shaped public perception and understanding of extraterrestrial life, influencing both individual and collective beliefs. Science fiction narratives have provided a rich tapestry of themes regarding alien encounters, advanced technologies, and the potential for interstellar communication. These stories often blur the lines between imagination and reality, creating a fertile ground for individuals to construct their own interpretations of UFO phenomena. As a result, science fiction has not merely entertained; it has also fostered a belief system that invites people to explore the possibility of alien life as a viable explanation for unexplained experiences.

The proliferation of science fiction in literature, film, and television has contributed to a cultural lexicon that normalizes the concept of UFOs and extraterrestrials. Iconic works, such as Arthur C. Clarke's "2001: A Space Odyssey" and films like "Close Encounters of the Third Kind," have provided audiences with narratives that suggest the existence of advanced civilizations. These representations often depict extraterrestrials as benevolent beings who seek to enlighten humanity, thereby promoting a worldview that is open to the idea of contact with alien entities. This narrative framework has proven influential in shaping the beliefs of those who may be predisposed to UFO cults and new religious movements.

Furthermore, the psychological impact of science fiction cannot be overlooked. The genre taps into fundamental human questions about existence, purpose, and the cosmos. As individuals engage with these speculative scenarios, they often find themselves contemplating their own beliefs about spirituality and the universe. This introspection can lead to a heightened interest in UFO-related phenomena and a willingness to explore alternative belief systems that align with the themes presented in science fiction. Thus, the genre serves as a catalyst for individuals seeking meaning, often pushing them toward UFO cults that promise answers to their existential inquiries.

The rise of social media has further amplified the influence of science fiction on UFO beliefs. Platforms like YouTube and Twitter allow for rapid dissemination of UFO-related content, including fan theories, personal testimonies, and speculative discussions. This environment encourages community building among those who share an interest in extraterrestrial life, often mirroring the communal aspects found in traditional religions. As individuals engage with these online communities, they may find themselves more susceptible to adopting the beliefs espoused by cult leaders who leverage the themes popularized in science fiction to attract followers.

In conclusion, the influence of science fiction on UFO beliefs is both profound and multifaceted. It shapes cultural narratives, informs personal beliefs, and fosters communities that explore the intersection of the known and the unknown. As new religious movements continue to emerge, fueled by these fictional narratives, it becomes essential to understand the psychological and social dynamics at play. By examining this connection, researchers and enthusiasts can gain deeper insights into the mechanisms that drive individuals toward UFO belief systems, ultimately enriching the discourse surrounding the phenomenon of alien messiahs and their followers.

THE ROLE OF MEDIA IN SHAPING PERCEPTIONS

The media plays a crucial role in shaping public perceptions of UFO phenomena and the cults that emerge around them. With the advent of both traditional and social media, narratives surrounding extraterrestrial life have proliferated, influencing individual beliefs and societal attitudes. Documentaries, news reports, and online forums serve as platforms for information dissemination, often framing UFO sightings and alien encounters in ways that resonate with existing cultural myths and fears. The portrayal of these phenomena can either validate or debunk beliefs, significantly impacting the growth and legitimacy of UFO-related religious movements.

Television shows and films have long depicted alien encounters as either harbingers of doom or benevolent beings seeking to assist humanity. This dichotomy shapes how individuals internalize their experiences and beliefs regarding UFOs. The sensationalization of sightings can create a heightened sense of urgency and significance around these events, prompting individuals to seek out communities or cults that offer explanations and solace. The emotional resonance of these media portrayals often leads individuals to align themselves with groups that provide a sense of belonging and purpose in a world filled with uncertainty and existential dread.

Social media platforms have emerged as vital arenas for the expression and reinforcement of UFO beliefs. Groups dedicated to discussing sightings, sharing personal experiences, and promoting new religious movements centered around alien encounters thrive in these digital spaces. The immediacy and accessibility of social media allow for rapid dissemination of information, enabling the formation of echo chambers where individuals can find affirmation of their beliefs. This phenomenon fosters a sense of community among members, which can further entrench their commitment to the group's ideology, often blurring the lines between rational discourse and fervent dogma.

The historical context of media's influence on cults emphasizes the cyclical relationship between technology, communication, and belief systems. From the early days of radio broadcasts that fueled the panic surrounding UFO sightings to the current viral nature of social media posts, each technological advancement has played a role in shaping the collective consciousness regarding extraterrestrial life. As new forms of media continue to evolve, they contribute to the ongoing narrative of alien messiahs, often leading to the emergence of new cult leaders who capitalize on these narratives to attract followers seeking answers to life's profound questions.

Understanding the role of media in shaping perceptions of UFO-related beliefs necessitates a critical analysis of the narratives being promoted. The ethical implications of these portrayals are significant, as they can inadvertently legitimize harmful ideologies or foster paranoia and distrust in established institutions. As disclosure enthusiasts and alien researchers explore this landscape, it becomes imperative to scrutinize the impact of media representations on individual psychology and group dynamics within UFO cults. By examining these influences, we can gain deeper insights into the intersection of belief, identity, and the allure of the unknown in contemporary society.

SPIRITUALITY IN THE CONTEXT OF SCIENCE FICTION

Spirituality within the realm of science fiction often serves as a compelling framework for exploring broader existential questions and humanity's place in the universe. In the context of UFO beliefs, science fiction narratives not only reflect societal anxieties about the unknown but also provide a rich tapestry for new spiritual movements. As these narratives evolve, they influence the development of belief systems that intertwine with traditional religious frameworks, often leading to the emergence of cults that draw on the allure of extraterrestrial encounters and the promise of higher consciousness.

The rise of cults and new religious movements surrounding UFO phenomena can be seen as a reaction to the profound questions and uncertainties posed by science fiction. These groups often adopt elements from popular culture, merging them with spiritual ideologies that resonate with their followers. For instance, characters and themes from science fiction literature and cinema frequently find their way into the dogmas of these cults, serving as modern mythologies that offer explanations for existential dilemmas. In this way, science fiction becomes a tool for articulating spiritual experiences that are otherwise difficult to express in conventional religious terms.

Moreover, the influence of UFO sightings on new religious movements highlights a growing desire for understanding and connection in an increasingly complex world. Many followers of UFO-based religions report transformative experiences that mirror the transcendent moments often depicted in science fiction narratives. These experiences can foster a sense of community among believers, as they collectively interpret their encounters as signs of a greater cosmic purpose. The intersection of these personal testimonies with the themes of science fiction allows for a rich exploration of spirituality that transcends traditional religious boundaries.

Social media plays a pivotal role in amplifying the spiritual aspects of UFO beliefs, facilitating the rapid dissemination of ideas and connecting individuals with similar interests. Online platforms enable the formation of virtual communities where members share experiences, rituals, and interpretations of science fiction as it intersects with their spiritual journeys. This digital landscape not only promotes the growth of UFO-related religious groups but also influences the psychological profiles of their leaders, who often harness these narratives to establish authority and legitimacy within their communities.

Finally, examining the rituals and practices of UFO-based religions reveals a fascinating blend of science fiction and spirituality. These rituals often incorporate elements of traditional religious practices while adapting them to fit the extraterrestrial narrative. This syncretism speaks to a broader trend where followers seek to integrate the spiritual insights gleaned from both ancient religions and modern science fiction. As the landscape of belief continues to evolve, the ongoing dialogue between spirituality and science fiction will undoubtedly shape the future of UFO cults and their impact on contemporary society.

Chapter 9

Examining the Practices of UFO-Based Religions

COMMON RITUALS AND THEIR MEANINGS

Rituals within UFO-based religions serve as powerful tools for reinforcing group identity and shared beliefs among members. Common practices often include group meditations, star-gazing events, and communal gatherings where followers share their personal experiences with extraterrestrial encounters. These rituals create a sense of belonging and foster a collective consciousness that aligns with the group's overarching narrative of alien contact. For many participants, these activities not only strengthen interpersonal bonds but also validate their beliefs in a broader cosmic plan, further entwining their identities with the cult's ideology.

One notable ritual observed across various UFO cults is the practice of channeling, where individuals claim to communicate with extraterrestrial beings or advanced spiritual entities. This process often involves a medium entering a trance-like state, during which they relay messages purportedly from aliens. The significance of channeling lies in its function as a bridge between the human experience and the alien realm, offering members a direct connection to what they perceive as higher knowledge. Such experiences are often framed as revelations, reinforcing the belief system of the cult and providing a profound sense of purpose to its members.

Another common ritual involves the use of sacred symbols and objects believed to possess otherworldly significance. These may include crystals, alien artifacts, or designated spaces where members feel a stronger connection to the extraterrestrial. The ritualistic use of these items often serves to enhance spiritual practices, such as meditation or prayer, creating a tactile link to their beliefs. By incorporating physical objects into their rituals, members imbue their practices with a sense of authenticity and urgency, reinforcing the idea that their path is not only spiritual but also rooted in tangible connections to the universe.

The timing of rituals often aligns with celestial events, such as meteor showers or planetary alignments, which are viewed as auspicious moments for communion with extraterrestrial forces. These events are frequently accompanied by elaborate ceremonies that blend traditional spiritual practices with contemporary interpretations of alien encounters. The synchronization with cosmic phenomena reinforces the belief that their actions are part of a larger universal rhythm, heightening the emotional investment of participants. This belief in cosmic timing elevates the significance of the rituals, making them more than mere gatherings; they become moments of profound spiritual engagement.

Finally, the impact of social media cannot be overlooked when examining the rituals of UFO cults. Platforms such as Facebook, Instagram, and YouTube provide avenues for disseminating ritualistic practices and sharing personal testimonies, which in turn attract new members and reinforce existing beliefs. Online communities often host live-streamed rituals, allowing individuals from around the world to participate and contribute to a global dialogue centered on UFO spirituality. This digital environment not only amplifies the reach of these groups but also shapes the rituals themselves, as members adapt their practices to fit the expectations and norms of an online audience. The interplay between traditional rituals and modern technology exemplifies the evolving nature of belief systems in the context of UFO disclosure.

THE ROLE OF GATHERINGS AND EVENTS

Gatherings and events play a pivotal role in the formation and sustenance of UFO-related cults, serving as crucial spaces for community building, collective experience, and the reinforcement of beliefs. These congregations often provide a sense of belonging for individuals who feel alienated from mainstream society, fostering an environment where shared experiences and narratives about extraterrestrial encounters can thrive. The rituals and activities conducted during these gatherings not only serve to strengthen interpersonal connections among members but also function as a means of affirming and propagating the cult's core doctrines. Through the lens of social psychological theories, one can observe how such events facilitate the creation of in-group identities, helping individuals find solace and validation in their beliefs.

The impact of these gatherings extends beyond mere socialization; they are instrumental in the psychological indoctrination of new members. During events, charismatic leaders often utilize persuasive techniques to reinforce their authority and the legitimacy of their teachings. This can involve dramatic storytelling, testimonials from alleged abductees, or even orchestrated experiences that simulate contact with extraterrestrial beings. Such tactics can create profound emotional responses among attendees, effectively deepening their commitment to the group's ideology. The collective nature of these experiences can lead to heightened states of suggestibility, making participants more susceptible to the beliefs being promoted by the cult leaders.

Moreover, gatherings and events serve as platforms for disseminating information, which can significantly influence the broader discourse surrounding UFOs and related phenomena. Cults often attract media attention during these events, allowing them to reach wider audiences and potentially recruit new members. The spectacle of large gatherings can generate intrigue, transforming the cult's narrative into a subject of public fascination. This visibility can result in a feedback loop, where increased media coverage leads to greater public interest and participation, further entrenching the cult within contemporary cultural discussions about extraterrestrial life and government disclosure.

The role of technology, particularly social media, cannot be overlooked in the context of these gatherings. Online platforms allow for the promotion and organization of events, facilitating connections among individuals who share similar interests in UFOs and related beliefs. As these platforms often blur the lines between virtual and physical gatherings, they enable cults to maintain engagement with their members and reach potential recruits who may not be able to attend in person. This intersection of online interaction and physical presence illustrates how modern communication tools enhance the cultivation of community and belief systems within UFO cults.

Ultimately, the dynamics of gatherings and events reveal significant insights into the psychology of cult membership in the context of UFO beliefs. The communal experiences fostered during these occasions are not merely social; they are vital to the psychological framework that underpins participation in such movements. By analyzing the rituals, interactions, and narratives shared in these settings, researchers can gain a deeper understanding of how alien messiahs exploit human psychology to create devoted followings. This exploration not only sheds light on the operational mechanisms within UFO cults but also raises important ethical questions regarding the influence of charismatic leadership and the nature of belief in the contemporary landscape of spiritual movements.

COMPARATIVE ANALYSIS OF PRACTICES

The examination of practices within UFO-based religions requires a comparative analysis that highlights both distinctive features and commonalities with traditional religious movements. In many cases, UFO cults exhibit a syncretic blend of established religious beliefs, science fiction narratives, and contemporary spiritual practices. This amalgamation allows for a unique framework in which followers find meaning and community, often drawing upon familiar motifs from mainstream religions while adapting them to the context of extraterrestrial belief systems. For instance, many UFO cults incorporate elements of apocalypticism, prophecy, and salvation narratives, paralleling themes found in major world religions, yet reinterpreted through the lens of extraterrestrial intervention.

A critical aspect of these practices is the role of charismatic leadership, which is prevalent in both UFO cults and traditional religious organizations. Cult leaders often present themselves as intermediaries between their followers and the alien beings they claim to contact, fostering a sense of exclusivity and urgency. This dynamic mirrors the authority structures in established religions, where spiritual leaders interpret sacred texts and provide guidance. The psychological profiles of these leaders reveal traits such as narcissism, grandiosity, and an ability to manipulate followers' emotions and beliefs, characteristics that resonate with those found in historical religious figures.

Rituals within UFO-centric groups can be compared to traditional religious practices, albeit with a distinctive focus on technology and extraterrestrial themes. For example, many cults engage in group meditations, channeling sessions, or public sightings designed to invoke a sense of connection with alien entities. These practices serve not only to solidify group identity but also to create an experiential framework where believers can feel the presence of the divine—or extraterrestrial—within their lives. This ritualistic element plays a crucial role in reinforcing communal bonds, establishing a shared narrative, and providing a framework for personal transformation that is reminiscent of initiation rites in various religions.

The impact of government disclosure on these movements further complicates the comparative landscape of UFO cult practices. Increased visibility and acknowledgment of unidentified aerial phenomena have led to a surge in interest and membership in UFO-related groups. This phenomenon can be likened to historical religious movements that gained momentum following significant societal changes or revelations. As disclosure initiatives unfold, cults often adapt their teachings and practices to align with new information, creating a feedback loop that intertwines belief, social dynamics, and external validations. The malleability of these practices highlights the fluid nature of beliefs in response to evolving societal narratives.

Lastly, the influence of social media cannot be overstated in the comparative analysis of UFO cults and traditional religions. Online platforms facilitate the rapid dissemination of information, allowing groups to recruit members and share experiences more effectively than ever before. The digital age has enabled a new form of community building that transcends geographical boundaries, allowing individuals to engage with UFO beliefs in ways that were previously impossible. This aspect emphasizes the evolving nature of spiritual practices, where traditional rituals may adapt or transform in response to the interactive and participatory culture of modern technology, further blurring the lines between established religious practices and the emergent rituals of UFO cults.

Chapter 10

Impact of Government Disclosure on Cult Membership

HISTORICAL INSTANCES OF GOVERNMENT DISCLOSURE

Historical instances of government disclosure regarding unidentified flying objects have significantly shaped the landscape of UFO beliefs and the subsequent rise of related cults and religious movements. One pivotal moment occurred in 1947, when the U.S. military recovered debris from what was initially reported as a "flying disc" in Roswell, New Mexico. The subsequent retraction of this statement and the introduction of the "weather balloon" narrative initiated a wave of speculation and conspiracy theories surrounding government secrecy and extraterrestrial life. This incident not only fueled public fascination with UFOs but also laid the groundwork for a distrust of government narratives that continues to resonate in contemporary discussions about extraterrestrial encounters.

Another significant episode in the history of government disclosure took place in the 1960s when Project Blue Book was established by the U.S. Air Force. This initiative aimed to investigate UFO sightings and determine whether they posed a threat to national security. Although Project Blue Book concluded that the majority of sightings could be explained by conventional means, its existence and the detailed reports generated contributed to a growing belief in the possibility of alien life. The project's findings and the eventual declassification of many documents allowed UFO enthusiasts and researchers to scrutinize government data, often leading to the conclusion that there was more to the story than was publicly acknowledged. This environment of selective transparency fostered the emergence of new religious movements centered around UFO beliefs.

The 1980s and 1990s witnessed a surge in government disclosures, particularly with the emergence of the Freedom of Information Act, which enabled researchers to access previously classified documents. This period resulted in significant revelations about military encounters with unidentified aerial phenomena. For many, these disclosures were seen as validation of long-held beliefs in extraterrestrial visitation, further solidifying the narratives propagated by various UFO cults. The relationship between these disclosures and the proliferation of cults during this era illustrates how official accounts can be interpreted and reinterpreted to fit the ideological frameworks of emerging religious movements.

In the modern context, the release of videos by the Pentagon showing encounters between Navy pilots and unidentified aerial phenomena in 2017 marked a significant turning point. This disclosure not only reignited public interest in UFOs but also legitimized some of the claims made by UFO researchers and enthusiasts. The acknowledgment of these phenomena by a government agency led to a spike in cult membership and interest in UFO-based spirituality, as individuals sought to make sense of these revelations through the lens of personal belief systems and communal narratives. The psychological impact of such disclosures often creates an environment ripe for cult formation, as individuals search for meaning in the face of perceived government obfuscation.

The intersection of government disclosure and UFO beliefs is further complicated by the role of social media in shaping contemporary narratives. As information spreads rapidly online, individuals are exposed to a multitude of interpretations of government disclosures. This democratization of information allows for the rapid formation of communities that coalesce around shared beliefs in extraterrestrial life and disclosure. The psychological profiles of cult leaders often reflect a keen understanding of these dynamics, cultivating a narrative that resonates with followers while exploiting the uncertainty surrounding government transparency. As historical instances of disclosure continue to influence the trajectory of UFO-related beliefs, they simultaneously illuminate the complex relationship between authority, belief, and the search for truth in the modern era.

CHANGES IN MEMBERSHIP DYNAMICS POST-DISCLOSURE

Changes in membership dynamics within UFO-related groups have become increasingly pronounced following significant government disclosures regarding unidentified aerial phenomena. These disclosures, often characterized by the release of previously classified information, have served as a catalyst for both the proliferation and evolution of new religious movements centered around extraterrestrial beliefs. The landscape of these movements has shifted, with existing groups experiencing fluctuations in membership, while new entities emerge to fill the void created by heightened public interest in UFOs and potential extraterrestrial life.

Post-disclosure, many established cults have reported an influx of new members, driven by a surge of curiosity and a desire for community among those seeking answers to existential questions surrounding the nature of humanity's place in the universe. This influx has often been accompanied by a diversification of membership demographics, with individuals from varied backgrounds and belief systems converging on these groups. The promise of exclusive knowledge about extraterrestrial beings and the supposed impending transformation of human society has proven to be an attractive proposition, drawing in seekers of truth and belonging.

Conversely, some groups have experienced significant attrition as members reassess their beliefs in light of new information. The revelations provided by credible sources can challenge the foundational tenets of certain cults, leading to disillusionment among followers who may feel that their leaders have misled them. This discontent can destabilize the internal dynamics of these groups, prompting leaders to adapt their narratives to retain followers. The psychological impact of disclosure on cult membership cannot be understated, as it forces both leaders and members to confront the implications of their beliefs in a rapidly changing context.

Social media has played a crucial role in re-shaping these membership dynamics, facilitating the rapid dissemination of information and fostering connections among like-minded individuals. Online platforms provide a space for discussions, testimonies, and the sharing of experiences, which can either reinforce existing beliefs or encourage individuals to seek new affiliations. As the discourse around UFOs and extraterrestrial life becomes increasingly mainstream, the boundaries between traditional religious practices and UFO cult beliefs blur, creating new hybrid forms of spirituality that attract diverse audiences.

In summary, the effects of government disclosures on membership dynamics within UFO-related groups are multifaceted and complex. The interplay of increased interest, shifting beliefs, and the influence of digital communication has transformed the landscape of these movements. As the phenomenon of UFOs continues to gain traction, understanding these changes becomes critical for researchers and enthusiasts alike, providing insight into the broader implications of belief systems in contemporary society.

THE FUTURE OF CULTS IN LIGHT OF CONTINUED DISCLOSURE

The future of cults in the context of ongoing disclosure regarding unidentified aerial phenomena (UAP) presents a complex landscape for both researchers and enthusiasts. As governments around the world begin to release previously classified information about UAP sightings and encounters, the potential for new religious movements centered around these phenomena becomes increasingly pronounced. The revelations serve not only as a catalyst for existing beliefs but also as a fertile ground for the emergence of new groups that may seek to interpret these disclosures through a spiritual or religious lens. This trend raises critical questions about the psychological profiles of cult leaders who may exploit such situations to gain influence and control over vulnerable individuals seeking understanding in a rapidly changing world.

The influence of UFO sightings on new religious movements has historically been significant, with prior instances of mass sightings leading to the formation of dedicated groups. As disclosure continues, it is likely that we will witness a resurgence in the formation of such movements, particularly among those disillusioned with traditional religious structures. These new groups may adopt unique theological frameworks that incorporate elements of science fiction and spirituality, appealing to a generation that increasingly looks to the cosmos for answers. Understanding the psychological motivations behind the leaders of these cults will be essential in comprehending how they can effectively communicate their messages and attract followers during periods of heightened interest in extraterrestrial life.

Social media plays a crucial role in the promotion and dissemination of UFO-related religious beliefs. Platforms that allow for the rapid sharing of information have the potential to amplify the reach of cults, enabling them to connect with a global audience. In this digital age, charismatic leaders can utilize social media to curate their narratives, drawing in individuals who resonate with their interpretations of UFO phenomena. This connectivity can create echo chambers where beliefs are reinforced, often leading to a radicalization of thought. As the phenomenon evolves, it is imperative to analyze how these platforms facilitate the growth of such movements and the implications for both individual followers and society at large.

Comparative studies of traditional religions and UFO cult beliefs reveal interesting parallels, particularly in how both systems address existential questions and the search for meaning. Many UFO cults incorporate rituals and practices reminiscent of established spiritual traditions, adapting them to fit their unique frameworks. Such practices might include communal gatherings, visionary experiences, or the use of symbolic artifacts, which serve to solidify the group's identity and belief system. As disclosure continues to unfold, these rituals may evolve further, potentially leading to a more mainstream acceptance of UFO-related beliefs within the broader spiritual landscape.

The impact of government disclosure on cult membership trends is an area ripe for exploration. As credible information about UAPs becomes more accessible, it may attract individuals who are curious yet skeptical about conventional explanations. This influx of new members could shift the dynamics within existing cults or lead to the formation of entirely new groups. Ethical implications arise from the potential exploitation of individuals seeking community and answers during times of uncertainty. It is essential for researchers and disclosure enthusiasts to remain vigilant about the psychological and societal ramifications of UFO cults as they navigate this uncharted territory, ensuring that the pursuit of knowledge does not come at the expense of vulnerable populations.

Chapter 11

Personal Testimonies of UFO Cult Members

QUALITATIVE ANALYSIS OF MEMBER EXPERIENCES

Qualitative analysis of member experiences within UFO-related cults provides a rich tapestry of personal narratives that illuminate the psychological and sociocultural dynamics at play. Members often report transformative experiences that align closely with their beliefs about extraterrestrial life and cosmic significance. These narratives frequently include initial encounters with UFO phenomena, which serve as catalysts for deeper exploration into alien ideologies. Such experiences often resonate with broader themes of existential searching, where individuals grapple with life's meanings and seek belonging within these communities.

The motivations driving individuals to join UFO cults vary significantly, often reflecting personal insecurities or crises. Many members express feelings of alienation from mainstream society, leading them to seek solace in groups that offer alternative explanations for their experiences and beliefs. This sense of belonging is reinforced through communal rituals and shared narratives that validate individual experiences of the extraordinary. As members recount their journeys, they frequently highlight the role of charismatic leaders who frame their experiences within a larger cosmological context, thereby enhancing the perceived legitimacy of their beliefs.

Moreover, the emotional landscape of cult membership is marked by a blend of hope, fear, and commitment. Members often experience a profound sense of purpose stemming from their belief in a mission to prepare for an impending cosmic event or transformation. This anticipation can create a euphoric sense of unity, yet it also engenders significant anxiety, particularly in the face of external skepticism or governmental interventions. Personal testimonies reveal how these emotional highs and lows contribute to a complex identity formation process, as members navigate their understanding of self in relation to both their peers and the outside world.

The impact of social media cannot be understated in shaping member experiences and facilitating community bonding. Digital platforms serve as vital spaces for sharing testimonials, discussing beliefs, and disseminating information about sightings and events. This modern form of congregation allows members to maintain connections beyond physical gatherings, fostering a sense of global community that transcends geographical boundaries. As individuals share their experiences online, they not only reinforce their beliefs but also attract new members who may resonate with these narratives, creating a feedback loop that strengthens group cohesion.

In summary, qualitative analysis reveals that member experiences in UFO cults are deeply intertwined with personal identity, emotional fulfillment, and communal belonging. The interplay of individual narratives and group dynamics illustrates the profound psychological impacts of these belief systems. By understanding the nuances of these experiences, researchers can better grasp the broader implications of UFO cults in contemporary society, particularly as they relate to psychological well-being, social cohesion, and the challenges posed by government disclosure and societal skepticism.

THE PSYCHOLOGICAL IMPACT OF CULT MEMBERSHIP

The psychological impact of cult membership, particularly in the context of UFO beliefs, is profound and multifaceted. Individuals drawn to these groups often experience a deep sense of belonging and purpose, which can be particularly compelling in an era marked by social dislocation and existential uncertainty. Cult leaders frequently exploit these vulnerabilities, positioning themselves as intermediaries between members and extraterrestrial entities. This dynamic fosters an environment where members feel validated in their beliefs, creating a reinforcing loop that deepens their commitment to the group.

Members often undergo significant cognitive and emotional transformations as they become entrenched in the cult's ideology. This can include a shift in identity, where personal beliefs and values become subsumed by the collective narrative of the group. The phenomenon of cognitive dissonance plays a crucial role here; as members encounter evidence contradicting their beliefs, the psychological discomfort often leads them to double down on their convictions. This reinforces their loyalty to the cult and its leader, making it increasingly difficult to extricate themselves from the group, even in the face of mounting external skepticism.

Isolation is another critical aspect of the psychological impact. Cults frequently employ strategies that sever members from their previous social networks, creating an echo chamber where only the group's beliefs are validated. This isolation can lead to an intense dependency on the group for emotional and social support, further entrenching members in their beliefs. The shared experiences of perceived alien encounters and revelations about supposed extraterrestrial agendas can create a strong sense of camaraderie among members, which can be psychologically intoxicating but also deeply harmful.

The rituals and practices of UFO-based religions often serve to reinforce psychological bonds among members. These rituals may involve communal gatherings, meditation, and other forms of spiritual practice that elevate the group's beliefs to a transcendent level. Such experiences can produce feelings of euphoria and a heightened sense of reality that members interpret as validation of their beliefs. This can create a cycle where the emotional highs associated with these practices further solidify their commitment to the group and its leader, making it increasingly challenging to question or abandon these beliefs.

Finally, the impact of government disclosure regarding UFOs plays a crucial role in shaping cult membership trends. As official narratives around UFOs shift, individuals seeking answers may turn to cults that provide a framework for understanding these phenomena. This intersection of belief, identity, and external validation creates a fertile ground for cults to thrive. The psychological ramifications of this dynamic are significant, as they not only affect individuals but also contribute to broader societal perceptions of reality and truth, highlighting the need for critical examination of both personal beliefs and collective narratives surrounding UFOs and alien encounters.

STORIES OF TRANSFORMATION AND BELIEF

Stories of transformation often serve as powerful catalysts for belief, particularly in the realm of UFO-related cults. Individuals drawn into these movements frequently undergo profound shifts in their personal narratives, embracing new identities that align with the teachings of their leaders. This transformation typically begins with a sense of disillusionment or dissatisfaction with conventional belief systems. Many members report feeling alienated from mainstream society, prompting them to seek solace and meaning in alternative frameworks. Through these experiences, they find a renewed sense of purpose that redefines their understanding of existence, often framed within the context of extraterrestrial encounters and cosmic revelations.

Central to these transformations are the charismatic leaders who wield considerable influence over their followers. These figures often present themselves as enlightened beings with direct connections to alien civilizations, claiming to possess exclusive knowledge about humanity's place in the universe. This perceived access to higher truths fosters a deep sense of trust and loyalty among members, who become willing to surrender their previous identities in favor of the transformative narratives propagated by their leaders. As they engage more deeply with these teachings, members often report experiencing spiritual awakenings, which reinforce their commitment to the group and its beliefs.

Personal testimonies from former cult members reveal the profound impact of these transformative experiences. Many recount moments of epiphany, where seemingly mundane events take on significant cosmic meaning, signaling their chosen status within the group. These narratives often include vivid descriptions of encounters with extraterrestrial beings or visions of an impending shift in human consciousness. Such experiences not only validate the teachings of their leaders but also create a shared sense of destiny among followers, further solidifying their bonds and deepening their commitment to the group's mission.

The role of social media in these transformations cannot be overlooked. Platforms like Facebook, Twitter, and Instagram provide fertile ground for the rapid dissemination of UFO-related ideologies and personal stories. This digital landscape allows individuals to connect with like-minded peers, share their experiences, and reinforce their beliefs in ways that traditional communities may not facilitate. The immediacy and accessibility of online interaction can amplify feelings of belonging and validation, making it easier for individuals to embrace transformative narratives and align themselves with the cult's objectives.

As we examine these stories of transformation and belief, it becomes evident that they reflect broader themes within the intersection of spirituality, psychology, and societal change. The allure of UFO-related cults often lies in their promise of a new reality, one that offers answers to existential questions and a sense of community. However, these narratives also raise ethical considerations regarding the manipulation of vulnerable individuals seeking meaning and connection. Understanding the psychological underpinnings of these transformations is crucial for disclosure enthusiasts and researchers, as it sheds light on the complex dynamics at play in the formation and sustenance of UFO-inspired belief systems.

Chapter 12

Ethical Implications of UFO Cults

THE ETHICAL DILEMMAS FACED BY CULT MEMBERS

The ethical dilemmas faced by cult members often revolve around the tension between personal beliefs and the demands imposed by the group. As these individuals become increasingly enmeshed in the doctrines of a UFO-based religion, they may find themselves grappling with conflicting values. Loyalty to the group often necessitates the suppression of personal doubts and ethical concerns, leading to a complex internal struggle. Members may rationalize their participation in controversial practices or the acceptance of dubious beliefs, which can create a dissonance between their innate moral compass and the expectations of the cult.

Manipulation and coercion are prevalent issues within many UFO cults, forcing members to confront ethical questions regarding their autonomy and the authenticity of their experiences. Leaders often exploit psychological vulnerabilities, using techniques such as love bombing and isolation from outside influences to reinforce their control. This manipulation can lead to profound ethical conflicts, as members must weigh their desire for belonging against the realization that their agency is being compromised. The emotional toll of such coercive dynamics often leaves individuals questioning the morality of their loyalty to the cult, even as they become further entrenched in its ideology.

Moreover, the promise of enlightenment or salvation associated with UFO beliefs can lead members to endorse actions they might otherwise find objectionable. This is particularly evident in cases where cults demand financial contributions or labor from their followers, often justifying these demands as necessary sacrifices for the greater good. Members may wrestle with the ethical implications of their contributions, especially when the benefits do not materialize as promised. This disparity between expectation and reality can foster feelings of guilt and complicity, prompting profound ethical reflections on the nature of their commitment to the group.

The question of informed consent also emerges in the context of UFO cults, particularly regarding the dissemination of information and the transparency of the group's activities. Many cults operate in secrecy, often withholding crucial details that could inform members' decisions about their involvement. This lack of transparency raises significant ethical concerns, especially when it comes to the potential risks associated with cult membership. Members may find themselves entangled in activities that conflict with their ethical principles, driven by a desire to fulfill perceived obligations to the group or its leaders.

Ultimately, the ethical dilemmas faced by cult members reflect broader societal issues related to authority, belief, and personal agency. As UFO cults continue to proliferate, understanding the ethical implications of their practices becomes increasingly important. Disclosure enthusiasts and alien researchers must consider how these dilemmas not only affect the individuals involved but also influence the public perception of UFO-related movements. Engaging with these ethical questions can facilitate a deeper understanding of the psychological and social dynamics at play within these groups, fostering a more nuanced discourse around the intersection of belief systems and ethical considerations in contemporary society.

SOCIETAL RESPONSES TO UFO CULTS

Societal responses to UFO cults are multifaceted, often oscillating between skepticism, fear, fascination, and engagement. As UFO sightings proliferated and the discourse surrounding extraterrestrial life gained traction, various segments of society began to grapple with the implications of these beliefs. Skeptics often deride cults as fringe groups, fueled by delusion and misinformation. This dismissal, however, overlooks the psychological and sociocultural factors that contribute to the emergence of these movements. When groups assert that they possess knowledge of alien beings or advanced civilizations, they tap into deep-seated human desires for connection, understanding, and transcendence.

The rise of UFO-related cults has been accompanied by a palpable shift in societal attitudes. Some communities have responded with curiosity, leading to increased engagement with the narratives and rituals of these groups. This interest often manifests in the form of media coverage, academic inquiry, and even participation in cult activities. Documentaries and exposés frequently romanticize the allure of UFO cults, presenting them as unique expressions of spiritual search rather than mere aberrations. Consequently, such portrayals can normalize these beliefs, encouraging a more nuanced understanding of the psychological profiles of cult leaders and their followers.

Moreover, the intersection of social media and UFO cults has significantly influenced public perception and engagement. Online platforms have become critical arenas for the dissemination of information, allowing cult leaders to cultivate communities and share their narratives with a global audience. These digital spaces often foster both support and dissent, enabling members to bond over shared beliefs while also inviting scrutiny from outsiders. The viral nature of social media can amplify the reach of UFO cults, leading to increased visibility and, in some cases, heightened controversy as traditional religious groups and skeptics respond to the challenge posed by these new belief systems.

The impact of government disclosure on cult membership trends is another important aspect of societal responses. As official narratives surrounding UFOs evolve, some individuals feel validated in their beliefs, while others may experience disillusionment. Government acknowledgment of unidentified aerial phenomena can lend credence to the claims of UFO cults, potentially attracting new members who seek community and purpose in the face of uncertainty. This dynamic creates a cyclical relationship, where increased visibility for UFO beliefs influences societal perceptions and, in turn, shapes the evolution of these cults.

Finally, personal testimonies and experiences of UFO cult members reveal the profound emotional and psychological dimensions of their involvement. Many members report transformative experiences that challenge their previous worldviews, reinforcing their commitment to the group. These narratives often highlight the search for meaning and belonging that drives individuals toward such movements. As society grapples with the implications of these beliefs, it becomes essential to consider the ethical dimensions of UFO cults, particularly concerning the vulnerability of individuals seeking solace in these alternative spiritualities. Understanding societal responses to UFO cults aids in unraveling the complex relationship between belief, community, and the human experience in the context of the unknown.

RECOMMENDATIONS FOR UNDERSTANDING AND ENGAGEMENT

To foster a deeper understanding and engagement with the phenomena surrounding UFO-related cults, it is essential for disclosure enthusiasts and alien researchers to approach the subject with a multifaceted perspective. This involves a careful analysis of the psychological profiles of cult leaders who exploit the allure of extraterrestrial narratives. By examining the motivations, backgrounds, and techniques employed by these individuals, researchers can better grasp how charismatic authority and persuasive communication shape the beliefs and behaviors of followers. Understanding these profiles can inform strategies to counteract manipulation and promote critical thinking within communities interested in UFO phenomena.

Engagement with the broader implications of UFO sightings on new religious movements is equally crucial. Historical analysis reveals that significant sightings often coincide with the emergence of new belief systems. Researchers should investigate the sociocultural contexts that give rise to such movements, considering factors like societal anxieties, technological advancements, and the quest for meaning in an increasingly complex world. By contextualizing UFO encounters within these frameworks, scholars can better appreciate how these events catalyze spiritual awakenings and the formation of cult-like groups.

The role of social media in promoting UFO-related religious groups cannot be overstated. Platforms such as Facebook, Twitter, and Instagram have transformed how information disseminates and how communities form around shared beliefs. Engagement strategies should focus on how these platforms can be used to disseminate accurate information, debunk myths, and support individuals questioning their involvement in such groups. Researchers might consider collaborations with tech companies to develop tools that identify and counteract misinformation while fostering healthy discourse among enthusiasts.

Comparative studies of traditional religions and UFO cult beliefs present an opportunity to explore commonalities and divergences in practices, rituals, and worldviews. Researchers should delve into the ways these new belief systems adopt and adapt elements of established religions, examining the psychological and social needs they fulfill. This comparative analysis can shed light on the underlying mechanisms that drive individuals to seek solace and community in both traditional and new religious contexts, ultimately enriching the discourse surrounding spirituality and belief in the modern era.

Finally, personal testimonies and experiences of UFO cult members serve as invaluable data for understanding the human dimension of these movements. Researchers should prioritize collecting narratives that highlight the emotional and psychological journeys of individuals involved in these groups. Ethical considerations are paramount in this endeavor, as it is vital to approach such stories with sensitivity and respect. By amplifying these voices, scholars can illuminate the complexities of belief, identity, and community, fostering a more nuanced under-

standing of the impact of UFO cults on contemporary society.

Chapter 13

Conclusion and Future Directions

SUMMARY OF KEY FINDINGS

The exploration of UFO-related cults reveals significant insights into the psychological profiles of their leaders and the broader societal implications of these movements. One of the key findings indicates that many cult leaders in the UFO belief system exhibit traits commonly associated with charismatic authority. These leaders often possess a profound ability to articulate a vision that resonates with followers' desires for meaning, belonging, and understanding in an increasingly complex world. Their narratives frequently incorporate elements of fear and hope, effectively mobilizing individuals who feel alienated or disenfranchised.

Another critical aspect uncovered through this analysis is the impact of historical UFO sightings on the formation of new religious movements. The cyclical nature of reported sightings has provided fertile ground for the emergence of cults that capitalize on the human fascination with extraterrestrial life and the unknown. This historical context underscores how collective experiences of perceived encounters with the extraterrestrial can catalyze the creation of belief systems that offer explanations for existential questions and societal anxieties.

The role of social media has been identified as a transformative factor in the proliferation of UFO-related religious groups.

Platforms such as Facebook, Instagram, and YouTube enable leaders to disseminate their messages widely and foster community among followers, transcending geographical boundaries. This digital engagement not only amplifies the reach of these movements but also allows for real-time interactions that reinforce group cohesion and validate individual experiences. The findings suggest that social media serves as both a recruitment tool and a space for ritualistic expression among adherents.

A comparative analysis of traditional religions and UFO cult beliefs reveals intriguing parallels and divergences in their structures and practices. While traditional religions often rely on established doctrines and sacred texts, UFO cults frequently emphasize personal revelation and direct experiences with the extraterrestrial. This distinction points to a broader trend where individuals seek spiritual fulfillment outside conventional religious frameworks, suggesting a shift in how spirituality is defined and experienced in contemporary society.

The implications of government disclosure regarding UFOs have also emerged as a significant factor influencing cult membership trends. As official narratives around UFO sightings evolve, individuals may gravitate towards groups that offer alternative interpretations and narratives that align with their beliefs about extraterrestrial life. This dynamic raises ethical considerations regarding the responsibilities of both leaders and researchers in navigating the psychological vulnerabilities of followers. Understanding these findings can contribute to a more nuanced perspective on the intersection of belief, authority, and the quest for truth in the context of UFO-related cults.

THE FUTURE OF UFO BELIEFS AND CULTS

As we look toward the future of UFO beliefs and the potential rise of associated cults, it becomes crucial to consider the ongoing evolution of societal attitudes toward unidentified aerial phenomena. This transformation is largely influenced by the increasing acceptance of UFO narratives in mainstream media and the scientific community. The recent acknowledgment of unidentified aerial phenomena by governmental bodies has catalyzed interest, leading to a surge in public curiosity. This newfound openness facilitates the emergence of new religious movements centered around extraterrestrial themes, leveraging the ambiguity of UFO phenomena to address existential questions and spiritual needs.

The psychological profiles of cult leaders within this context reveal a distinctive interplay between charisma, belief systems, and social dynamics. Many leaders exploit the current cultural zeitgeist surrounding UFOs, positioning themselves as intermediaries between humanity and higher extraterrestrial intelligences. They often draw upon a blend of science fiction and spiritualism, appealing to individuals seeking meaning in an increasingly complex world. This confluence of psychological manipulation and social validation can lead to the rapid growth of these groups, as followers find solace in shared beliefs and communal experiences centered on UFO phenomena.

Historical patterns suggest that as UFO sightings increase, so too does the formation of new religious movements. Previous decades have illustrated how significant sightings or events can serve as catalysts for cult formation. The future may see a similar trajectory, with increased government transparency and ongoing public fascination fueling the development of new doctrines and practices. These movements often reflect broader societal anxieties, including fears of technological domination and environmental collapse, positioning extraterrestrial beliefs as a source of hope or salvation.

The role of social media cannot be understated in this context. Platforms for sharing information and personal experiences provide fertile ground for the propagation of

UFO-related ideologies. As individuals increasingly turn to online communities for connection and validation, these groups can leverage social media to recruit and maintain membership. The immediacy of online communication allows for rapid dissemination of beliefs, rituals, and narratives that reinforce a collective identity. This digital landscape creates an environment where UFO cults can thrive, adapting to contemporary culture while reaching global audiences.

Lastly, the ethical implications of the rise of UFO cults warrant careful examination. As more individuals gravitate toward these movements, the potential for exploitation increases, particularly for vulnerable populations seeking answers or belonging. The intersection of psychological need and charismatic leadership can lead to detrimental outcomes for followers. It becomes essential for researchers and disclosure enthusiasts to critically assess the impact of these groups on individuals and society, ensuring that the pursuit of knowledge regarding UFOs does not come at the cost of personal autonomy or well-being. The future of UFO beliefs, therefore, rests not only in the events of the skies but also in the ethical stewardship of the narratives that emerge on Earth.

FINAL THOUGHTS ON THE INTERSECTION OF UFOS AND SPIRITUALITY

The intersection of UFOs and spirituality presents a complex landscape shaped by historical narratives, psychological factors, and sociocultural dynamics. As UFO sightings gain prominence, they often transcend mere curiosity, evolving into profound spiritual experiences for many individuals. This phenomenon is evident in the emergence of new religious movements that intertwine extraterrestrial beliefs with traditional spiritual practices, often positioning UFOs as messengers or manifestations of a higher consciousness. The psychological profiles of cult leaders in this context reveal a unique blend of charisma and conviction, enabling them to attract followers seeking meaning in an increasingly uncertain world.

Cult leaders often exploit the allure of UFO phenomena to construct elaborate belief systems that resonate with the spiritual aspirations of their adherents. These leaders frequently present themselves as intermediaries between humanity and advanced extraterrestrial beings, promoting a narrative that not only addresses existential questions but also offers a sense of community and belonging. The psychological underpinnings of these movements are steeped in the need for connection and understanding amid societal disillusionment, thus fostering environments where followers may be more susceptible to manipulation and indoctrination.

Historically, the rise of UFO-centric cults has mirrored societal anxieties and technological advancements. From the post-war era to the digital age, each wave of UFO sightings has been accompanied by a surge in groups claiming divine connection with alien entities. This historical analysis underscores the cyclical nature of belief, where the intersection of science fiction and spirituality becomes a fertile ground for new religious ideologies. As such, the role of social media in disseminating these beliefs cannot be underestimated, allowing for rapid propagation and recruitment that challenges traditional notions of religious authority and community formation.

The rituals and practices of UFO-based religions often reflect syncretic blends of established religious traditions and novel extraterrestrial mythologies. These practices serve not only as expressions of faith but also as mechanisms for reinforcing group identity and solidarity among members. Personal testimonies from individuals within these cults reveal the deeply personal nature of their experiences, highlighting how the promise of extraterrestrial encounters can fulfill spiritual needs that are often unmet within conventional religious frameworks. Such narratives contribute to our understanding of the broader implications of these movements on individual psychology and societal norms.

As discussions surrounding government disclosure and its effects on UFO cult membership trends continue to evolve, it is crucial to critically examine the ethical implications of these beliefs. The potential for exploitation within these groups raises significant questions about the responsibilities of researchers, policymakers, and society at large. As the boundaries between spirituality, belief, and psychological manipulation blur, a nuanced understanding of the intersection of UFOs and spirituality becomes essential for fostering informed dialogue and promoting ethical considerations within the growing field of UFO studies.